CANADA
the land

Bobbie Kalman

A Bobbie Kalman Book

The Lands, Peoples, and Cultures Series

Crabtree Publishing Company
www.crabtreebooks.com

The Lands, Peoples, and Cultures Series
Created by Bobbie Kalman

For Dean,
who loves Canadians, eh?

Written by
Bobbie Kalman

Coordinating editor
Ellen Rodger

Editor
Jane Lewis

Contributing editors
Carrie Gleason
Heather Macrae

Editors/first edition
Janine Schaub
David Schimpky
Lynda Hale

Production coordinator
Rose Gowsell

Design and production
Text Etc.

Separations and film
Quadratone Graphics Ltd.

Printer
Worzalla Publishing Company

Photographs
Gillian Bailey/Anne Gordon Images: p. 19 (bottom);
Marc Crabtree: p. 27 (top); Betty Crowell: p. 19 (top);
Stephen Dunn/International Exposure: p. 23 (top);
Robert Estall/Corbis/Magmaphoto: p. 21; Ken Faris:
p. 13 (bottom); Anne Gordon/Anne Gordon Images:
cover, p. 3, 25 (bottom right); Robert Holmes/
Corbis/Magmaphoto: p. 10 (bottom); Industry,
Science, and Technology Canada: p. 20 (inset), 23
(bottom), 24, 25 (bottom left), 26, 28; Wolfgang
Kaehler: title page, p. 4, 8, 9 (both), 10 (top), 11
(bottom), 13 (top), 15 (top), 18 (bottom),
22 (left), 27 (bottom), 29 (top left and right), 30
(both), 31 (bottom); James Kamstra: p. 20; Stephen
J. Krasemann/Photo Researchers: p. 12, 29 (bottom
right); Pat & Tom Leeson/Photo Researchers: p. 29
(bottom left); Diane Payton Majumdar: p. 11 (top);
Milt & Joan Mann/Cameramann Int'l., Ltd.: p. 22
(right), 25 (top); Ontario Ministry of Tourism and
Recreation: p. 6; Ron Schroeder: p. 17 (bottom),
18 (top); Jim Steinberg/Photo Researchers: p. 7;
Dave Taylor: p. 31 (top left and right); other
images by Digital Stock

Every effort has been made to obtain the appropriate credit
and full copyright clearance for all images in this book. Any
oversights, despite Crabtree's greatest precautions, will be
corrected in future editions.

Map
Jim Chernishenko

Illustrations
Scott Mooney: icons
David Wysotski, Allure Illustrations: back cover

Cover: A field of commercial sunflowers grows
in Ontario.

Title page: Lunenburg, Nova Scotia, is an important
fishing port on Canada's east coast.

Icon: A loon is a swimming bird found in northern
Canada.

Back cover: Caribou are large deerlike animals that
roam Canada's north.

Published by
Crabtree Publishing Company

PMB 16A,	612 Welland Avenue	73 Lime Walk
350 Fifth Avenue	St. Catharines	Headington
Suite 3308	Ontario, Canada	Oxford OX3 7AD
New York	L2M 5V6	United Kingdom
N.Y. 10118		

Cataloging in Publication Data
Kalman, Bobbie, 1947 -
 Canada. The land / Bobbie Kalman.--Rev. ed.
 p. cm. -- (The lands, peoples, and cultures series)
 Includes index.
 Summary: Describes the geography, natural resources, trade
and industry, cities, people, transportation, agriculture, and
environment of Canada.
 ISBN 0-7787-9358-3 (RLB) -- ISBN 0-7787-9726-0 (pbk.)
 1. Canada--Juvenile literature. 2. Canada--Geography--
Juvenile literature. [1. Canada.] I. Title. II. Series.
 F1008.2 .K35 2002
 971--dc21

 2001032526
 LC

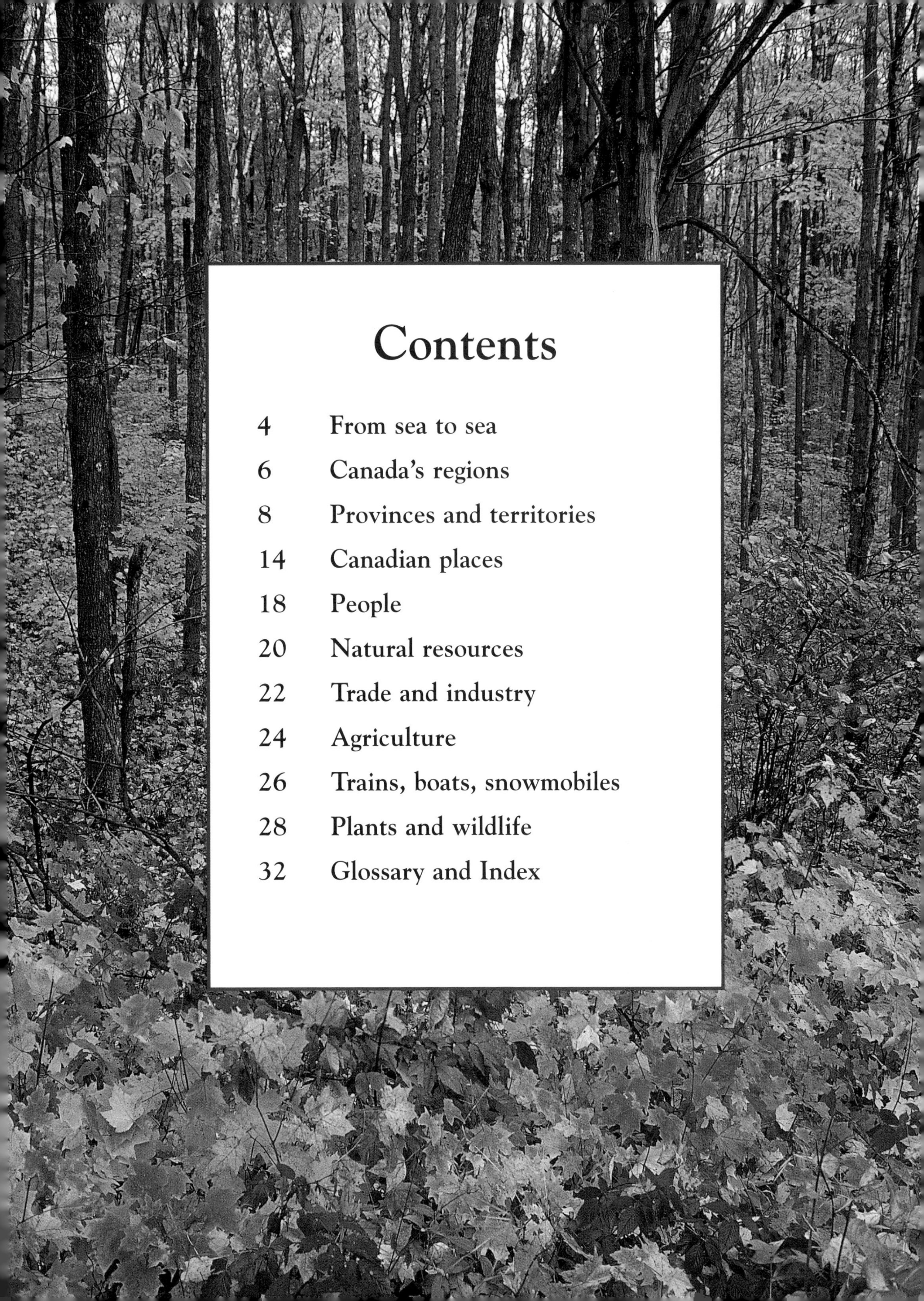

Contents

4   From sea to sea

6   Canada's regions

8   Provinces and territories

14   Canadian places

18   People

20   Natural resources

22   Trade and industry

24   Agriculture

26   Trains, boats, snowmobiles

28   Plants and wildlife

32   Glossary and Index

From sea to sea

Canada covers most of the northern part of North America. It is the second largest country in the world, after Russia. Canada's national motto "from sea to sea" describes a land that stretches from the Atlantic Ocean in the east to the Pacific Ocean in the west. The northern border of Canada reaches to the Arctic Ocean and the southern border meets the United States. The Canada–United States border is the longest undefended national border in the world.

The work of the glaciers

Thousands of years ago, most of Canada was covered by large rivers of ice, called **glaciers**. As the glaciers spread across Canada, the force of their weight carved and shaped the land. When the glaciers retreated, hills, valleys, and ridges were left. Holes and **gullies** in the earth were filled with **meltwater**, creating lakes and rivers. Over the centuries, plants, animals, and people have made this rugged land their home.

A diverse land

Canada is geographically diverse, meaning that it is made up of many different physical regions. There are coastal areas, vast forests, mountain regions, arctic **tundra**, and **prairie** grasslands. These dramatic differences in geography cause weather conditions to be extremely different from place to place. On the same day that a person in southern Ontario is sizzling in a heat wave, someone in Iqaluit may be tracking through the snow. Most Canadians live in areas with **temperate** conditions, where freezing winters give way to mild springs, hot summers, and cool autumns.

(below) The remains of a glacier that shaped Moraine Lake in Alberta still exists on the tops of surrounding mountains.

(opposite page, top) Glaciers can be seen in many of Canada's scenic national parks.

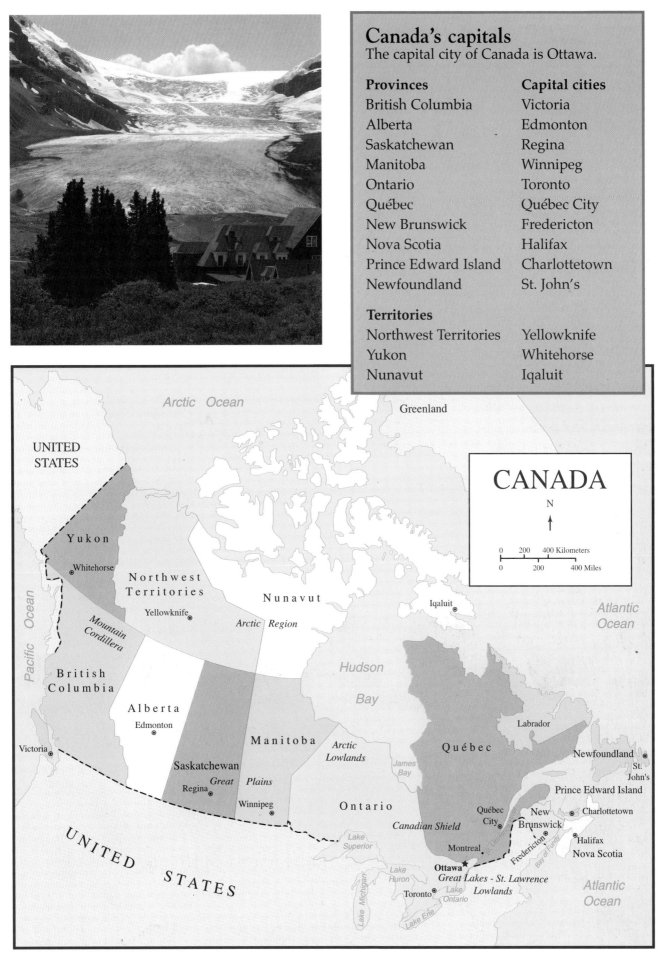

Canada's capitals
The capital city of Canada is Ottawa.

Provinces	Capital cities
British Columbia	Victoria
Alberta	Edmonton
Saskatchewan	Regina
Manitoba	Winnipeg
Ontario	Toronto
Québec	Québec City
New Brunswick	Fredericton
Nova Scotia	Halifax
Prince Edward Island	Charlottetown
Newfoundland	St. John's

Territories	
Northwest Territories	Yellowknife
Yukon	Whitehorse
Nunavut	Iqaluit

Arctic Ocean

Greenland

UNITED
STATES

CANADA

N
↑

| 0 | 200 | 400 Kilometers |
| 0 | 200 | 400 Miles |

Yukon

Whitehorse

Northwest
Territories

Nunavut

Yellowknife

Iqaluit

Atlantic
Ocean

Pacific Ocean

Mountain
Cordillera

Arctic Region

British
Columbia

Alberta

Edmonton

Hudson

Bay

Labrador

Victoria

Saskatchewan

Manitoba

Arctic
Lowlands

Québec

Newfoundland

St.
John's

Regina

Great Plains

Winnipeg

James
Bay

Ontario

Prince Edward Island

Québec
City

New
Brunswick

Charlottetown

UNITED

Canadian Shield

Fredericton

Halifax

Lake
Superior

Montreal

Bay of Fundy

Nova Scotia

STATES

Ottawa ★

Great Lakes - St. Lawrence
Lowlands

Atlantic
Ocean

Lake
Michigan

Lake
Huron

Toronto

Lake
Ontario

Lake Erie

Canada's regions

One way to get a clear picture of Canada's geographic diversity is to divide the country into seven regions:

1. The Appalachian Region
2. The Canadian Shield
3. The **Great Lakes**–St. Lawrence Lowlands
4. The Arctic Lowlands
5. The Great Plains
6. The Mountain Cordillera Region
7. The Arctic Region

The Appalachian Region

The Appalachian Region covers the provinces of New Brunswick, Nova Scotia, Prince Edward Island, Newfoundland, and a portion of Québec south of the St. Lawrence River. This region is a mixture of rocky shoreline, sandy beaches, rich farmland, and thick forests. The hills and valleys of this region were created by ancient volcanic activity.

The Canadian Shield

The Canadian Shield covers nearly half of Canada. This region includes Labrador, most of Ontario and Québec, and the northern part of Manitoba and Saskatchewan. The Canadian Shield, also called the Precambrian Shield, was formed two and a half billion years ago by glaciers. It consists of bare rock, thick forests, and cold freshwater lakes. In fact, this region contains one-quarter of the world's fresh water!

(below) Glaciers carved the landscape of the Canadian Shield, which covers much of Canada. Most of the Canadian Shield is blanketed by forests. In autumn, the leaves of many of these trees turn spectacular colors of orange, red, and yellow.

The Lowlands

The Great Lakes–St. Lawrence Lowlands are located between the Canadian Shield and the north shores of Lake Ontario, Lake Erie, and the St. Lawrence River. This region is home to most of Canada's large cities and industries. With its fertile farmlands and many industries, this region is often referred to as "Canada's heartland." While the region does include some long ridges of high ground, such as the Niagara Escarpment, the landscape is generally flat.

The Arctic Lowlands

The extreme north of Ontario and Manitoba around Hudson Bay is the region known as the Arctic Lowlands. The land in this region is mainly flat and marshy, and supports little vegetation. The area is sparsely inhabited and attracts few visitors, with the exception of Churchill, Manitoba.

The Great Plains

The Great Plains run through Manitoba, Saskatchewan, and parts of Alberta. This region, formerly grasslands, is famous for grain farming and cattle ranching. The Great Plains, also known as the prairies, contain a wealth of **natural resources,** such as minerals, oil, and natural gas.

The Mountain Cordillera

The region covering British Columbia, the Yukon, and parts of Alberta is called the Mountain Cordillera. The Rocky Mountains and the Coastal Mountains are part of this region. The Mountain Cordillera also boasts rainforests with thousand-year-old trees and valleys that are ideal for growing fruit. Hundreds of islands can be found off the Pacific coast of British Columbia. With the exception of Vancouver Island, many of these islands are small and uninhabited.

The Arctic Region

The far north of Canada is called the Arctic. This region is characterized by mountains, frozen oceans, and barren tundra. The northernmost part of the region is the Arctic **Archipelago**, a group of islands located in the Arctic Ocean. Summer in this region lasts only a couple of months. The Arctic winter is long, dark, and extremely cold.

(above) Waterton Lakes National Park in Alberta is the only place in Canada where the prairie landscape directly meets the mountains. In most areas, there are foothills between the flat plains and the rugged Rockies.

7

 Provinces and territories

Canada is divided into ten provinces and three territories. Newfoundland, Prince Edward Island, Nova Scotia, and New Brunswick are known as the Atlantic provinces, or Atlantic Canada. Québec and Ontario are called central Canada. Manitoba, Saskatchewan, and southern Alberta are called the prairie provinces. British Columbia and parts of Alberta are called the western provinces, or western Canada. The Yukon, the Northwest Territories, and Nunavut are referred to as Canada's northern territories.

Newfoundland

Canada's easternmost province consists of a mainland area, called Labrador, and a large island. Together they make up the province of Newfoundland. Newfoundland was originally settled by Europeans who fished for cod in the Atlantic Ocean. Today, most Newfoundland residents live on the island's coasts. Many fisheries have been shut down, but fishing is still a large part of the culture of the province.

Prince Edward Island

Canada's smallest and most **densely populated** province is Prince Edward Island. Sandstone cliffs, green fields, sandy white beaches, and rolling hills can be found throughout the province. Its warm climate and rich red soil are well suited for farming. The eight mile (12.9 kilometer) Confederation Bridge, built in 1997, connects Prince Edward Island to mainland New Brunswick. In winter, it is the longest bridge over ice-covered water in the world!

Scenic Nova Scotia

Nova Scotia means "new Scotland," and this province looks a lot like the country after which it was named. Misty highlands, flower-filled valleys, and old villages are all part of Nova Scotia's landscape. Cape Breton Island, rugged and mountainous, is also part of this province.

(above) Small fishing villages, such as Peggy's Cove, line the coasts of Nova Scotia.

New Brunswick

Forests cover 80 percent of New Brunswick. The rest of the countryside is a combination of mountains, plains, marshes, and rugged coastline. Sandy beaches and salmon-fishing rivers are found on the eastern shores of the province. The Bay of Fundy, a large **inlet** that separates Nova Scotia from New Brunswick, has the world's highest **tides**. The water level in the bay can rise 52 feet (16 meters)!

Unique Québec

Québec is Canada's largest province. Its name comes from the native Algonquin word "Kebec," meaning "where the river narrows." It is here that the Gulf of St. Lawrence narrows to the St. Lawrence River. The province has fertile farmlands, coniferous forests, and mountains. Eighty percent of Québec's population is francophone, or French speaking, giving the province a personality and culture distinct from the rest of Canada.

(right) Niagara Falls is also called the Horseshoe Falls because of its shape. It attracts almost twelve million visitors every year.

(below) The lush, rolling farmland of Québec.

Bustling Ontario

Ontario is Canada's second largest province. It is also the wealthiest province and has the largest population. The name Ontario comes from a native Iroquois word meaning "beautiful water." Lakes and rivers occupy one-sixth of Ontario's area. Niagara Falls, one of the seven natural wonders of the world, is located on Ontario's southern border. The thundering water of Niagara Falls drops 176 feet (54 meters)!

Manitoba

Open grasslands dominate the south of Manitoba, forests are in the middle, and bush and tundra cover the northern part of the province. Manitoba's climate ranges from arctic-like winters to warm summers. Winnipeg, the capital city, is a major cultural center known for its music and **multicultural** festivals. The northern town of Churchill on Hudson Bay attracts many visitors because of its intriguing wildlife—polar bears!

Prairie Saskatchewan

The name of this province comes from a native Cree word meaning "swiftly flowing river." Saskatchewan has many rivers and more than 100,000 lakes. It also has rocky areas, forests, and large stretches of prairie farmland. This province grows the most wheat in North America. Saskatchewan grain is exported to countries all over the world.

(above) Polar bears make their home in the arctic landscape of northern Manitoba.

(below) The vast, flat prairies of Saskatchewan are ideal for growing wheat and other grain crops.

(top) Alberta and British Columbia share the Rocky Mountains, one of Canada's spectacular wilderness areas.

(bottom) Lush rainforests are part of British Columbia's varied landscape. Many old-growth forests, such as this one, are being clearcut because of the logging industry.

Alberta's variety

Alberta is the westernmost of the prairie provinces but it also has mountains, exciting cities, and untouched wilderness. Saskatchewan and Alberta share the **badlands**, an area of barren, arid land containing rock formations, called **hoodoos**. Alberta has some of the world's richest deposits of fossils and dinosaur bones. The province is also known for an interesting winter weather phenomenon called the chinook. A chinook is a warm, dry wind that blows off the Rocky Mountains. It can melt a prairie snow cover in just a few hours.

Beautiful British Columbia

British Columbia is known as "Canada's playground." Most of the province is covered by forests and mountains. Lakes, a desert, coastal islands, **rainforests**, and vast areas of wilderness are also part of the landscape. The Okanagan Valley in south central British Columbia offers orchards filled with apples, apricots, peaches, cherries, and grapes. The city of Victoria, on Vancouver Island, is the capital of British Columbia.

11

The Yukon

The Yukon Territory lies between the Northwest Territories and the American state of Alaska. The Yukon is about one-third of the size of Alaska, and is almost entirely covered with mountain ranges. Visitors are attracted to the beautiful scenery of this territory to camp, hike, canoe, and fish.

The Northwest Territories

The Northwest Territories is among the area known as "the land of the midnight sun." This is because areas north of 67 degrees latitude experience 24 hours of sunlight during the short summer season. Although there are some mountains and forests, this territory is mostly barren tundra. The Northwest Territories once stretched between the Yukon and Hudson Bay. In 1999, it was divided and the eastern region of the Northwest Territories became a new territory called Nunavut.

Nunavut

On April 1, 1999, a long-time dream of the **Inuit** people of the Canadian north became a reality. Nunavut, Canada's first self-governed native territory, was created. Nunavut means "our land" in Inuktitut. Inuktitut is the language of the Inuit people, who make up 83 percent of the population of the territory. Nunavut contains vast stretches of tundra and polar islands, covering an area twice the size of Ontario.

(above) Kluane National Park is located in the southwest corner of the Yukon. It covers 8,494 square miles (22,000 square kilometers) of land.

12

Permafrost

The land of Canada's northern territories is covered in permafrost. Permafrost is soil that is always frozen. Only a thin top layer of earth thaws during the summer. Permafrost prevents most trees and plants from growing because their roots cannot grow deep into the frozen earth.

Anyone for pingo?

What looks like a volcano but has a core of ice? If you said an Arctic pingo, you would be right! Pingos are large hills of soil and ice. A pingo is formed when a small frozen lake is covered by a thin layer of soil. The lake water freezes under the soil, expanding upward to form a hill on the land. The earth that covers the pingo prevents the ice underneath from melting. At the top of the pingo the soil is easily blown off by the wind. When the sun shines, the uncovered ice melts and leaves a depression. This depression looks like the crater of a volcano.

(above) Grise Fjord is a small village on Ellesmere Island, an island of Nunavut. The arctic region of Canada has little vegetation because the ground is always frozen.

(below) Most pingos are found around the mouth of the Mackenzie River. Pingos are large hills of soil and ice that are thousands of years old.

The majority of Canadians live in or around **urban centers**. More than one-third of Canada's population lives in the country's three largest cities: Toronto, Montréal, and Vancouver. Ottawa is the nation's capital. Many other places, including Dawson City and Head-Smashed-In, tell interesting stories about Canada's past.

Toronto

With a population of close to five million people, Ontario's capital city is Canada's largest city. Toronto is also the fourth largest city in North America. It is a major center for banking, manufacturing, communications, business, arts, and culture. The city has many art galleries, theaters, and museums. Various music and multicultural festivals take place throughout the year. Two famous Canadian structures, the CN Tower and the SkyDome, are in Toronto. The CN Tower is the largest free-standing structure in the world. The SkyDome is a sports complex famous for its roof, which opens and closes.

Montréal

Montréal is in the province of Québec. It is Canada's second largest city and the second largest French-speaking city in the world, after Paris. Montréal was founded in 1642 by the French, and was originally called Ville Marie. The old part of the city is located on an island in the St. Lawrence River on an extinct volcano called Mont Royal. Montréal is a major port and center for business, finance, fashion, and transportation. Montréal is also Canada's center for French arts and culture. It is famous for its annual jazz and comedy festivals.

(below) Toronto's CN Tower and SkyDome are distinct features of the city's skyline. The city is located on the shore of Lake Ontario.

Ottawa

In the early nineteenth century, Ottawa was a small logging settlement called Bytown. Its present name, Ottawa, comes from a native Algonquin word meaning "to trade," because the area was once a major trading center for some native groups. The city was chosen as Canada's capital by Queen Victoria when Canada was a colony under British rule. With about one million residents, Ottawa is the fourth largest city in Canada. The Canadian Parliament buildings and government offices are located in Ottawa. Ottawa is located on the border between Ontario and the mostly French-speaking province of Quebec, which makes it a **bilingual** city. The Canadian government encourages all of its workers to speak both French and English.

(below) The Canadian Parliament buildings in Ottawa overlook the Rideau Canal. In the winter months, the canal becomes the longest outdoor skating rink in the world!

Vancouver

Canada's third largest city is in southern British Columbia. With the Pacific coast on one side and the Coastal Mountains on the other, Vancouver is surrounded by beauty. Natural areas can be found within the city as well. Stanley Park, in downtown Vancouver, covers 1000 acres (405 hectares) of land and features hiking trails, a zoo, an aquarium, and beaches. This west coast city is known as a major center for tourism, arts, fashion, business, industry, sports, and film-making. People from all over the world have settled in Vancouver. The city has the largest Asian population in North America.

(above) Vancouver is Canada's third largest city, located on Canada's west coast.

Historic Québec City

Settled in 1608, Québec City is one of Canada's oldest cities and Québec's capital. The historic section of the city is surrounded by stone walls. Inside the walls, narrow cobblestone streets are lined with colorfully painted shop fronts. Artists, jugglers, and street musicians show off their talents to interested tourists. A large hotel called the Château Frontenac dominates the city. Outside the city walls is the newer part of town, where most of the residents live.

Head-Smashed-In Buffalo Jump

Head-Smashed-In might seem like a strange name for a place, until you hear its history! Eleven miles (18 km) northwest of Fort Macleod, Alberta, Head-Smashed-In Buffalo Jump is the world's oldest, largest, and best preserved buffalo jump. A buffalo jump is a place where native people chased buffalo over a cliff. The buffalo fell to their death below, where native peoples would then carve the buffalo for food. It is a famous place that shows what life was like for the native peoples long ago.

Dawson City

Dawson City, in the Yukon Territory, was a native fishing camp until 1896. In that year, gold was discovered and the **Klondike Gold Rush** began. Dawson City became a popular destination for fortune seekers, and the city was nicknamed the "Paris of the North." By 1898, Dawson City was the largest city in western Canada, with more than 30,000 inhabitants. The city had telephones, running water, and **steam heat**—all luxuries at the time. The gold rush lasted only a few years, and when it ended, people left Dawson City by the thousands. Today, the population is about 2,000 people. Tourism and gold mining are Dawson City's major industries.

(opposite page) A castle-like hotel called the Château Frontenac in Québec City.

(below) Head-Smashed-In Buffalo Jump was once used for hunting buffalo by native people.

People

Canadians can trace their ancestry to every continent of the world. Native peoples have lived in Canada for thousands of years. Over the past 500 years, immigrants from all over the globe have made Canada their home, creating a truly multicultural nation.

First People

The first people in Canada were the native peoples. They came from Siberia 40,000 years ago by crossing a land or ice bridge that stretched across the Bering Strait. By the time Europeans arrived in the sixteenth century, native groups had spread across the country and established languages, customs, religious beliefs, laws, and governments. Today, there are about 500,000 native people in Canada. There are also about 450,000 Métis, who are people of mixed native and European ancestry.

(above) Canada's 31 million people come from a variety of backgrounds.

(right) There are about 600 Native Canadian bands, or groups, in Canada.

Immigrants

In the sixteenth century, Europeans came to Canada to fish for **cod** off the Atlantic coast. The fishing and later fur trade industries led to permanent French and British settlements. Over the next few centuries, waves of immigrants from countries such as Germany, Scotland, Ireland, Italy, the Ukraine, Holland, Greece, Poland, and Scandinavia also made Canada their home. More recently, immigrants have come from South East Asia, Africa, South America, and the Caribbean. Today, most Canadians can trace their ancestry to one or many of these groups.

In the past twenty years, Canada has adopted a more open immigration policy. Immigrants from all over the world make Canada their home. Many immigrants settle in the larger cities, such as Toronto and Vancouver, where there are more job opportunities. Canada also accepts refugees from around the world. Refugees are people escaping harsh conditions, war, or persecution in their own country. Most recently, refugees from the war-torn areas of Europe have come to Canada for safety and protection.

Multiculturalism

In 1971, Canada became the first country in the world to adopt an official policy on multiculturalism. The policy states that all Canadian people are legally equal, no matter what their race, origin, or religion. The policy is designed to make sure that all Canadians can keep their cultural identities, take pride in their ancestry, and still have a sense of belonging to Canada.

Two official languages

Canada has two official languages—English and French. Nearly a hundred other languages are spoken, including approximately 53 native languages. Chinese is the third most commonly spoken language in Canada, followed by Italian, German, and Spanish.

(above) Canada is officially a bilingual country. In some areas, both languages appear on signs.

(below) Large Canadian cities, such as Toronto and Vancouver, have areas called Chinatown.

 # Natural resources

Canada is famous for its wealth of natural resources. It has more fresh water, trees, and fish than any other country in the world. Trees, fish, animals, water, minerals, and fuels are examples of raw materials that have been harvested, hunted, and mined in Canada for centuries. The three most valuable natural resources in Canada are natural gas, crude oil, and water.

Natural gas

Natural gas is a colorless, odorless **fossil fuel** found under the earth. When burned, natural gas creates less pollution than oil or coal. Natural gas is Canada's main source of energy. Most of Canada's natural gas comes from Alberta and is distributed through a huge system of pipelines across Canada and the United States.

Oil

Oil and gas are petroleum products. Petroleum is refined, or purified, and used to run cars, trucks, and planes. It is also used to make **asphalt** and plastics. Crude oil is a black liquid substance found under the earth. Most of Canada's crude oil comes from large deposits in Saskatchewan and Alberta. Nova Scotia and Newfoundland are also being developed as sources of oil. Canada is a major supplier of oil to the United States.

(above) Trees cover almost half of Canada. When cut down, trees supply lumber for building, pulp for papermaking, and wood to burn as fuel.

(inset) In Sudbury, Ontario, nickel is mined from large deposits in the earth. Coal, zinc, copper, and iron are also mined in Canada.

A valuable natural resource

The Great Lakes, Hudson Bay, and countless other freshwater lakes and rivers make up a large portion of Canada's area. Canada has more fresh water than any other country in the world. Fresh water is a valuable natural resource. Waterways played a part in Canada's history, providing transportation and trade routes for native peoples and early European explorers. Today, the St. Lawrence Seaway and the Great Lakes are still used for shipping.

Water power

Large dams on rivers provide **hydroelectricity** to homes and industries. Hydroelectricity uses fast water to drive **turbines**, which in turn create electrical power. Many people feel hydroelectricity is more beneficial than other energy sources because it produces less air pollution. But large dams also have negative effects. Dams are built to keep water from naturally flowing, creating a **reservoir**, which floods the surrounding land. This flooding can destroy animal and human **habitats**.

Renewable and non-renewable

There are two kinds of natural resources. Water, plants, and animals are renewable resources. If used carefully, nature will replace them: new trees grow, more animals are born. Substances that are mined from the earth, such as minerals, oil, and natural gas, are non-renewable resources. Once these resources are gone, they cannot be replaced for millions of years.

Dwindling resources

It is important to use non-renewable resources wisely, since they cannot be replaced once they are gone. It is also important to use renewable resources carefully. It takes time for nature to replace them, so these resources cannot be used up too quickly. For example, trees take hundreds of years to grow to full size.

One hundred years ago, cod was so plentiful off the coast of Newfoundland that people could reach into the water and scoop up a bucket full of fish. In 1992, the Canadian government noticed that the number of cod in the Atlantic Ocean had declined. The government passed a law stating that no one could fish the cod for a certain amount of time, so that the cod population could recover. Thousands of Newfoundlanders who depended on the cod fishing industry for a living were suddenly out of work.

(above) The St. Lawrence River is 800 miles (1,287 kilometers) long. The waterway has been called "the gateway to North America." The St. Lawrence Seaway is a series of canals, locks, and dams along the St. Lawrence River. It was built in the 1950s to allow ships to travel between the Atlantic Ocean and the Great Lakes. Ships can access both Canadian and American ports on the Great Lakes.

Trade and industry

The Canadian economy is made up of a wide variety of industries, from **agriculture** to tourism. Canadians mine minerals, make plastic, mill pulp and paper, grow food, produce chemicals, and extract petroleum. The three largest industries in Canada are mining, manufacturing, and services.

Resources and industry
Some of Canada's industries depend on the country's abundant natural resources. Industries that gather and sell natural resources, such as the fisheries and logging industries, are called primary industries. Industries that make goods from these raw materials, such as food processing plants and papermaking companies, are called secondary industries. The two industries rely on each other.

Loss of natural resources
Some primary industries in Canada are in danger because the country's natural resources are being used up too quickly. Overfishing has drastically reduced the number of fish in Canadian waters. This puts the fishing industry in danger. The lumber industry will suffer if Canada's forests are depleted. If the lumber industry fails, then numerous secondary industries that rely on pulp and paper will also fail.

Steel
Canada is one of the world's largest producers of steel. Iron ore, the raw material from which steel is made, is mined from the ground in Québec, Labrador, and British Columbia. Most iron and steel manufacturing takes place in Ontario.

Service with a smile
Canada's largest industry is the service industry. Its business is helping people. Banks, accounting firms, supermarkets, and health clubs all offer services to people. Some of these organizations are privately owned, others are operated by the government.

Tourism
Canada's cultural offerings and beautiful landscapes attract more and more tourists every year. Visitors come from all over the world. They spend money in hotels, restaurants, shops, theaters, museums, amusement parks, and on tours and transportation. This money helps the Canadian economy. The tourism industry provides jobs for thousands of Canadians.

(below) Three large American automobile manufacturers—General Motors, Ford, and Chrysler—have taken advantage of Canada's large supply of steel and built factories there. The factories provide jobs for many Canadians.

(left) The fishing industry in Newfoundland is in decline because the cod has been overfished.

(above)The logging industry is depleting one of Canada's important natural resources—its forests. Growing awareness of the problem has led to some improvement. For example, many logging companies now replant areas that they have harvested, so that new trees will grow for future generations.

Free trade

Many Canadian companies sell their goods to other countries. Companies from other countries sell goods to Canada. This exchange of goods is called trade. Canada trades most of its products with the United States. The North American Free Trade Agreement, also called NAFTA, was signed on Jan 1, 1994, by Canada, the United States, and Mexico. This agreement allows the countries to trade goods and services without having to pay extra taxes, called tariffs.

Some people believe that NAFTA has helped Canadians by increasing trade between countries and providing more business for Canadian companies. Others believe that NAFTA has hurt Canadian businesses because they cannot compete with the cheaper products and manufacturing costs of American and Mexican companies.

(above) Pulp and paper manufacturing is one of Canada's largest industries. It relies on forestry for its raw materials. Most pulp and paper mills are located in British Columbia, Ontario, and Québec.

Agriculture

About one thousand years ago, Native Canadians began planting and harvesting corn. They eventually grew beans and squash, and harvested wild rice. In later years, native peoples traded their extra **produce** with the European settlers. The settlers gradually cut down the huge forests that covered most of the countryside. They began to raise **livestock** and grow a variety of crops.

Fewer farmers

As recently as one hundred years ago, seven out of ten Canadian families worked in agriculture. Farms included many types of livestock and crops. Today, only one or two families in a hundred are farmers. Most farmers grow just one crop or raise one type of livestock. A farm in the prairies may grow only wheat, whereas a farm in Québec may raise only beef or dairy cattle.

Canada's crops

Canadians grow a variety of crops, such as wheat, barley, oilseed, tobacco, fruits, and vegetables. The Okanagan Valley in British Columbia and the Niagara region in southern Ontario produce apples, apricots, cherries, peaches, pears, grapes, and plums. Agriculture in the prairie provinces is devoted almost entirely to growing grain. The Annapolis Valley in Nova Scotia is famous for its apples. Prince Edward Island is known for producing potatoes—70 varieties, in fact!

Incredible canola

Canada is responsible for the development of canola. Canola is a grain that is grown mainly in western Canada. The seeds are crushed and processed into canola oil, which is one of the healthiest oils humans can use for cooking. After the oil is removed from the seeds, the leftover seeds are used to make products such as animal feed and fertilizer.

(above) Some farms specialize in raising dairy cows. Using modern equipment, the cows are milked several times each day. Cheese, sour cream, and yogurt are just a few products made from milk.

(right) Apples are grown in many areas of Canada. They are harvested from the trees in early autumn.

(below) In the summer, many children and adults pick strawberries from the fields in Ontario.

(opposite page) Beautiful yellow fields of canola plants can be found on the prairies.

Trains, boats, snowmobiles

Before the invention of automobiles, airplanes, and railways, traveling across Canada was quite difficult. With dense forests and no roads, progress was slow and treacherous. Native Canadians often traveled long distances on rivers and lakes in canoes. The Inuit used dogsleds and snowshoes to travel over the snow. Early Europeans arrived with horses and large sailing ships, but getting from place to place still took a long time.

The national dream

The invention of the steam engine, which was used to power trains, changed the way people traveled. Distances that once took weeks to cover now took just a few days. Sir John A. Macdonald, Canada's first **prime minister**, took on the project of building a railroad right across the country. This was known as "the national dream." Cutting across the rugged Canadian landscape was not an easy task, but the railway was finally completed in 1885. It played an important role in uniting Canada.

Modern rail travel

Today the Canadian government owns and operates most of the trains that travel the country's 22,370 miles (36,000 kilometers) of track. Recently, passenger service has been reduced to help the trains save money. However, rail travel is still popular with tourists and Canadian travelers who want to see the remote countrysides of Canada.

Shipping

Canada still relies on ships to carry goods across the country and around the world. Canada's major ports are Vancouver, Churchill, Toronto, Montréal, Québec City, Halifax, and St. John's. The St. Lawrence Seaway allows ocean-going ships to enter the heart of the commercial areas of the country. The St. Lawrence Seaway is about 2,400 miles (3,862 kilometers) long and is made up of a system of locks and canals.

(below) Taking the train is still a popular way to see Canada's natural beauty.

A very long highway

Canada has many roads and highways, which are used by Canada's 18,000,000 vehicles. The Trans-Canada Highway is the longest paved highway in the world. It extends 4,660 miles (7,500 kilometers) from St. John's, Newfoundland to Victoria, British Columbia.

(above) Automobile travel is the most popular mode of transportation in Canada.

(below) Ski-doos are used extensively in Canada's northern regions.

One Canadian's doo-ing

One Canadian man's vision resulted in the invention of a vehicle that can travel on snow. Born in Québec in 1908, J. Armand Bombardier spent his young adult years developing the Ski-doo, or snowmobile. In 1937, he created the first models, which were large and carried a number of passengers. These early snowmobiles were used mainly as medical vehicles. Today, Ski-doos are one- or two-passenger vehicles that are used for transportation and recreation. The Inuit in Canada use snowmobiles for daily transportation and hunting expeditions. Bombardier Incorporated remains a world leader in the manufacture of snowmobiles. The company also makes **all-terrain vehicles**, aircraft, boats, and rail vehicles.

 # Plants and wildlife

Canada is famous for its many types of wildlife and vast areas of wilderness. The coastal regions, the prairies, central Canada, and the arctic all provide different habitats for plants and animals. Some natural features are common across Canada. The Boreal Forest, a wide band of evergreen trees, stretches across all the provinces. Animals such as the beaver, one of Canada's national symbols, are found across the country.

Atlantic Canada

The Atlantic provinces have large forested areas that provide homes for hares, porcupines, and moose. Sea birds, such as puffins, blue herons, and terns, live on the coast. So many blue herons nest in the marsh areas of Prince Edward Island that the bird has been named the symbol of the province's national parks. Whales and seals can be seen in the waters off Newfoundland and Labrador. Also in coastal waters are colonies of mussels, clams, and lobsters. The Pitcher Plant grows in Newfoundland. It eats insects!

Central Canada

Large portions of Ontario and Québec are covered with spruce and fir trees. Foxes, lynx, raccoons, and bears can be found in these areas. Québec's Bonaventure Island is a world famous bird **sanctuary** and is home to thousands of gannets. Point Pelee, Ontario, is the most southern point of Canada, and the warmest part of Canada's mainland. It is a beautiful place when hordes of Monarch butterflies stop over during their migration to Mexico in September.

(above) The moose is a famous Canadian symbol. These herbivores can be found in most areas across Canada. A grown moose can weigh up to 1,800 pounds (820 kilograms).

The prairies

The prairie provinces were once covered with tall grasses. Now, farmers use most of the flat lands for growing wheat. The northern regions of the provinces are covered by Boreal forests, which are home to elk, bears, moose, and lynx. North of the forests are marshes and swamps, which are nesting grounds for several varieties of ducks and geese. Great Gray owls live in Manitoba. The owls hunt mice and rabbits at night.

(top left) Grizzly bears in western Canada can be as large as eight feet (2.5 meters) long. They can weigh as much as 900 pounds (410 kilograms).

(top right) The bald eagle is the largest bird of prey found in Canada. These impressive birds are seen mainly in western Canada.

(bottom left) The beaver is one of Canada's national symbols. Beavers live in almost every region of the country.

(bottom right) Many animals that live in the Arctic have natural camouflage. The white fur of this young harp seal blends into the snowy northern landscape.

29

Western Canada

The west coast of Canada is an area of mountains and rainforests. The Rocky Mountains provide shelter and food for moose, brown bears, caribou, elk, lynx, cougars, and mountain goats. Grizzly bears are also found in this region of the country. Whales, sea lions, and sea otters live along the coastline. Orcas, or killer whales, can be seen from whale-watching boats as they migrate along the Pacific Coast. Bald eagles also live near the coastal waters.

The Arctic

Canada's Arctic tundra is the area north of the **tree line**. Lichen, moss, shrubs, and some briefly blooming wildflowers are the only plant life in the Canadian Arctic. Some animals have adapted well to the habitat of this unforgiving landscape. Arctic foxes and hares live in the barren north. The Snowy Owl has a thick coat of feathers to help it survive the climate. White beluga whales spend their winters in the waters off Nunavut. Polar bears live in Manitoba, Labrador, and the Arctic regions of Canada. Polar bears have thick layers of fat and fur to insulate them from the bitter cold, and to help them float. These large animals can weigh up to 1200 pounds (544 kilograms)!

Canadian national parks

In many places, land has been set aside by the government to protect natural areas and wildlife species. These areas, called national parks, are great places to visit and learn about nature. Canada has 39 national parks. In addition, each province has many provincial parks. Hunting, mining, and logging are strictly limited in these areas. Canada is still working to designate certain areas as national parkland. When the parks program is complete, national parks will cover nearly three percent of Canada's area.

The first national park in Canada was Banff National Park. It was created in the 1880s when railroad workers discovered **hot springs** at the foot of Sulphur Mountain. Pelee Island National Park is Canada's most southern National Park. It is a migration stopover for thousands of birds that spend their winters in South America and their summers in Northern Canada. The Saguenay-St. Lawrence Marine Park in Québec protects eastern Canada's marine life, including whales, seals, and birds.

(above) Bonaventure Island in Québec is only 2.2 miles (3.5 kilometers) wide, but is a sanctuary to more than 200,000 birds!

(below) More than 50,000 gannets are part of Bonaventure Island's bird population.

Endangered species

Some plants and animals have become **endangered** due to overhunting and the destruction of their habitats. Laws restricting hunting and trapping have saved several species from extinction. Other problems affecting endangered animals, such as pollution and the growth of cities taking up animal habitat, are not easy to solve.

There are currently 353 plant and animal species on Canada's endangered list. If the **ecosystems** in which they grow and live are not protected, these species will become extinct. Some of the endangered species are the Peregrine Falcon, the Northern Sea Lion, the Bowhead Whale, and the Peary Caribou. Species such as the Great Plains Wolf and the Sea Mink are already extinct.

(top left) At one time sea otters were almost extinct. Now their ocean habitat is threatened by pollution.

(top right) Although western cougars are still common, the eastern cougar is believed to be extinct.

Old-growth forests

Some forests in Canada are full of trees that are hundreds of years old. These forests are known as old-growth forests. Unfortunately, many of these forests have been clearcut. Clearcutting means cutting down all the trees in an area, leaving the land barren. Logging companies now plant new trees where old forests have been cut down, but it is impossible to restore the original ecosystem of plants and animals. British Columbia is known for its impressive old-growth forests. The Western red cedar is just one example of the trees grown here. Some of these trees are 1000 years old.

(right) Red cedars can grow up to 200 feet (60 meters) tall!

Glossary

agriculture Farming

all-terrain vehicle A vehicle with three or four wide wheels used for driving over uneven ground

archipelago A group of islands

asphalt A black tar that, when mixed with sand or gravel, is used for paving roads

badlands A rocky region in Alberta with many ridges, peaks, and gullies, formed by erosion

bilingual Able to speak two languages

cod A species of fish found in the Atlantic Ocean

clearcut To chop down every tree in an area

densely populated Many people living in a small area

ecosystem A community of living things that are connected to one another and their environment

endangered species A group of animals or plants threatened with extinction

foothills Small hills at the base of a mountain range

fossil fuel A fuel such as petroleum, natural gas, or coal found deep beneath the earth

glacier A huge river of slowly moving ice

Great Lakes A group of five large freshwater lakes: Lake Ontario, Lake Erie, Lake Michigan, Lake Superior, and Lake Huron

gully A small trench or valley

habitat The living space of plants, animals, and people

hoodoo A rock formation shaped by wind and water

hot spring A place where unusually warm underground water flows out of the earth

hydroelectricity Electricity produced by waterpower

inlet A narrow body of water leading inland from a larger body of water

Inuit Native people who live in Canada's Arctic

Klondike Gold Rush When gold was discovered in the Klondike, an area of the Yukon, thousands of people rushed to the area hoping to make a fortune by mining the gold.

livestock Domestic animals such as cattle or pigs

meltwater Water from melting snow and ice

multicultural Of many cultures

natural resources Useful materials such as water, trees, and minerals that are found in nature

prairie A large treeless plain or grassland

prime minister The head of the Canadian government

produce Farm products such as fruits and vegetables

rainforest A dense forest that receives a great deal of rainfall

reservoir A pond or lake used for holding water

sanctuary A safe area where plants and animals are protected from human activity

steam heat Steam used to create heat energy

temperate Describing a climate that has no extreme highs or lows in its temperature

tide The regular rise and fall of water caused by the gravitational pull of the sun and moon

tree line The northern limit to which trees will grow

tundra A flat, treeless region in northern Canada

turbine An engine powered by a wheel that is turned by water, steam, or air

urban center A city

 # Index

agriculture 7, 8, 9, 10, 15, 22, 24–25, 29
Alberta 4, 5, 7, 8, 11, 17, 20, 30
Arctic 4, 6, 7, 10, 12, 13, 29, 30
Arctic Ocean 4, 7
Atlantic Ocean 4, 8, 21
Bay of Fundy 9
British Columbia 5, 7, 8, 11, 15, 22, 23, 25, 27, 31
Canadian Shield 6, 7
Cape Breton Island 8
cities 5, 10, 11, 14–17, 19, 20, 26, 31
CN Tower 14
Dawson City 14, 17
endangered species 31
farming *see* agriculture
fishing 8, 12, 17, 21, 22
forests 4, 6, 7, 9, 10, 11, 12, 20,

22, 23, 24, 26, 28, 29, 30, 31
geographical regions 6–7
Great Lakes 21
Halifax 5, 26
Head-Smashed-In 14, 17
industry 11, 21, 22–23
Iqaluit 4, 5
Labrador 6, 8, 22, 28, 30
Lake Erie 7
Lake Ontario 7, 14
Manitoba 5, 6, 7, 8, 10, 29, 30
Montréal 14, 26
NAFTA 23
national parks 4, 7, 12, 28, 30
native peoples 17, 18, 21, 24
natural resources 7, 20–21, 22, 23
New Brunswick 5, 6, 8, 9
Newfoundland 5, 6, 8, 20, 21,

22, 27, 28, 30
Niagara Falls 9
Northwest Territories 5, 8, 12, 13
Nova Scotia 5, 6, 8, 20, 25
Nunavut 5, 8, 12, 30
Ontario 4, 5, 6, 7, 9, 14, 15, 20, 22, 23, 25, 28
Ottawa 5, 14, 15
Pacific Ocean 4
people 18–19
Point Pelee 28, 30
prairies 4, 7, 8, 10 11, 24, 25, 28, 29
Prince Edward Island 5, 6, 8, 25, 28
provinces and territories 8–13
Québec 5, 6, 9, 14, 15, 16, 17, 22, 23, 24, 27, 28, 30

Québec City 5, 16, 17, 26
Rocky Mountains 4, 5, 7, 11, 30
St. John's 5, 26, 27
St. Lawrence River 6, 7, 14, 21
St. Lawrence Seaway 21, 26
Saskatchewan 5, 6, 7, 8, 10, 11, 20
Toronto 5, 14, 19
trade 22–23
transportation 21, 26–27
tundra 4, 7, 10, 12, 30
Vancouver 14, 15, 19, 26
Vancouver Island 7, 11
wildlife 4, 10, 28–31
Winnipeg 5, 10
Yukon 5, 8, 12, 17

1 2 3 4 5 6 7 8 9 0   Printed in the U.S.A.   9 8 7 6 5 4 3 2 1 0